Dreams of Natural Places

Dreams of Natural Places

A New England Schooner Odyssey

by Herbert Smith

A Peter Randall Book

Published by
Down East Books

Saint Georges' Harbor, Grenada, Windward Islands

For Tommy

© 1981 by Herbert Smith

Edited and designed by Peter E. Randall

Typesetting: A & B Typesetters
          Concord, NH
Color separations: Graphic Color Service
          Waterville, ME
Printing: George Little Press
          Burlington, VT
Binding: Robert Burlen & Son, Incorporated
          Accord, MA

Library of Congress Card Catalogue Number: 80-69529
ISBN: 0-89272-107-3

A Peter Randall Book

Published by Down East Books
          Camden, ME

Dominica, Windward Islands

Beauty, which is the most precious
thing in the world, at times lies
dormant, off the beaten track, waiting
to be discovered. It can go unnoticed
forever or sing its tune to those who
want to listen. It is a melody that
can fill your heart with serenity.

South Pacific

Squall line, South Pacific

Saint Barts

7

South Pacific

Off Bora Bora

North Atlantic

Contents

Indian Ocean

Foreword

In 1519, Charles V of Spain sent Magellan westward across the Atlantic in search of a route to the East Indies. At the coast of South America, Magellan sailed south until he reached the tip of the continent and discovered the strait that still bears his name. After winding through this strait, Magellan entered the ocean he named Pacific and, carried by the trade winds, sailed westward to Guam and the Philippines.

Magellan was killed by natives in the Philippines and the command of his ship was assumed by first officer Elcano. Following his dead commander's plans, Elcano continued with the voyage sailing through the East Indies, around the African Cape of Good Hope and home to Spain. This was the first voyage around the world and has been considered the greatest voyage of discovery of all time.

Since those early years, thousands of men and women have shared the fantasy of a round the world voyage but only a few people, including those who actually begin such a journey, ever complete the voyage. Four hundred and fifty nine years after Magellan, the 65-foot schooner *Appledore* with a crew of 15 began a cruise around the world, departing from Portsmouth, New Hampshire.

Many ships and crews had passed before and charted the route. Many sailors had become legends as a result of their quest. What their eyes beheld and their minds imagined has been written about many times, often enough to arouse a special yearning in others who sought to follow in their wake. However, rarely have sailors returned with visual impressions of their travels because few were artists and photography is only a recent development.

Dreams of Natural Places is a visual account of a round the world voyage and many of the scenes in this book are unchanged since the days of Magellan.

Acknowledgements

Without the help of many people, in particular the *Appledore* crew and the boat builders, the voyage would not have been possible.

I would especially like to thank my wife, Doris, who gave much support to the voyage and in the writing of the text of this book.

I would also like to thank Peter Randall for his encouragement of the book during the early stages of the voyage and for his work in producing the finished volume.

Appledore's Crew Members

Alexandria Clark	Tom Smith*
Dave Dash	Jack Stiles
Marion Dash	Maria Stiles
Margaret Gaeth*	Alan Twombly*
Mike Johnson	Donna Twombly*
Rita Kunkle	Greg Wellstead*
Kathy Mahany	Sandra Wellstead*
John Richards*	Anne Williams
Doris Smith*	Jack Williams

* crew members for the entire voyage

Passing Appledore Island, Isles of Shoals

A Beginning

Everyone has dreams. Some are fulfilled and others remain dreams. I am not sure whether it is better to fulfill a dream or just to have it.

My dream began twenty-seven years before *Appledore* was constructed. While growing up in Portsmouth, New Hampshire, I often passed the restored homes of sea captains such as John Paul Jones. Someday, I wanted to share in the romance of owning and captaining a traditional sailing vessel.

I had a couple of small boats when I was a teenager and one summer morning with a boyhood friend, Skipper Day, we sailed out to the Isles of Shoals. To us it was a great adventure. We knew little about the sea.

The Isles of Shoals is a group of small islands six miles from the mouth of Portsmouth Harbor. One island in the group is named Appledore. On that summer day, at our first sighting of Appledore, a lobsterman's small daughter waved from the doorway of her father's house. Little did she or I realize that we would meet again, that she would become my wife and that we would sail around the world together in a ship named for that island.

My dream grew throughout those boyhood years and it was reinforced by such things as a television series about the South Pacific called "Adventures in Paradise," and by seeing a lecture and meeting Captain Irving Johnson who sailed his famed schooner *Yankee* around the world several times.

I joined the Coast Guard after high school because I wanted to be stationed at the Portsmouth Harbor lifeboat station where I could continue to operate small boats. Instead I was assigned to the icebreaker *Eastwind* and sailed to Antarctica. In a remarkable coincidence, the icebreaker stopped at Pitcairn Island on the way south and, to my astonishment, there was Irving Johnson's schooner *Yankee*. This rare encounter truly set my mind to work on the goal of someday sailing around the world.

After leaving the Coast Guard, I spent some time in the Merchant Marines sailing across the Pacific. The long hours of inactivity provided ample time to dream and formulate means and ways to accomplish those dreams. The lack of financial resources did not allow me to seriously consider building a schooner and it was even longer before I began to gain the knowledge that was required to sail one. Upon returning to the States, I attended Brooks Institute of Photography and later pursued a career as a wildlife photographer which provided a substantial income and ultimately the wherewithal to pursue my dream.

During the summer months I returned to Portsmouth where I worked as a lobster fisherman. Here I met Doris Plante. We began dating but didn't realize until after we were married that we had met before. Doris was the little girl who had waved to me from the small house on Appledore island so many years earlier.

In December of 1978, with my wife and our 11-month old son, Tommy, I drove through Damariscotta, Maine with everything we owned piled in the back of our pick-up truck. We were on our way to South Bristol where *Appledore* was going to be built. We knew right off that we were going to like this part of Maine. The streets of Damariscotta were dressed out in genuine spruce wreaths and Christmas lights hung across the street. Snow was falling and the tires squeaked as they rolled over the newly fallen snow. I stopped on the side of the road to give the windshield wipers a snap to get the snow off, and with the wind blowing in around the open collar of my shirt, I found it hard to believe that next winter we would be sailing in the tropics.

Our rented house in South Bristol overlooked the Gamage shipyard and each morning, with snow crunching under our feet, it was only a short walk to work. Linwood Gamage, owner of the yard, had granted Doris and me permission to work alongside the regular crew. We hired a babysitter for Tommy and went to work. At 6:30 a.m., the old navy submarine dive alarm sounded to commence the day's activities. Leather drive belts began to slap as the machinery gained momentum and, combined with the smell of the wood burning stoves, we got in the right frame of mind to work on a traditional wooden schooner.

Prior to arriving in South Bristol, I had tramped the woods of New Hampshire with lumberman Lawrence Lyford. We selected the huge white oak trees for *Appledore*'s construction. Each tree was marked with a different colored ribbon and was carefully picked for a specific timber to be sawn.

Our work in the Gamage Shipyard was a challenging and interesting occupation for eight months. The shipyard had become famous for building many of the World War II minesweepers and new windjammers. The machinery had not changed for half a century. Huge ship's band saws could cut through a 12-inch white oak timber like a piece of cheese and the old timers like Earl, Hartwell, Jim and Brian knew how to handle a timber that size. Doris and I went home exhausted each evening, while they went out to moonlight on other jobs. Fortunately, we did not work weekends.

In February, a storm swept the Maine coast pushing the tides higher than ever before in history. Water actually came into the building and up under the keel. Everyone joked about an early launching, however, it would be many months before *Appledore* would be ready. Construction did move quickly, however. No one then knew I planned to sail the schooner around the world, yet nothing was spared to build the boat as strong as possible. By August, *Appledore* was ready to be launched, just three days before the yard was to close for summer vacation.

Launching a schooner in a traditional shipyard is exciting. First, a cradle is built under the vessel. The cradle rests on wooden planks which lead down to the water's edge. The planks get a heavy coat of grease and on high tide, when the restraints are cut away from the cradle, the vessel literally slips down the planks into the water, gaining momentum as it goes. The old timers say it is not a good launching unless the grease smokes. On August 22, 1978, after being christened with a bottle of champagne, *Appledore* did it properly. With grease smoking, she slid down the ways into the welcoming arms of the Atlantic Ocean. We set a departure date of November 9, 1978 to begin our voyage around the world. The dream was becoming a reality.

Appledore under construction. (above) Framing. (below right) Sawing timbers. (below left) Planking.

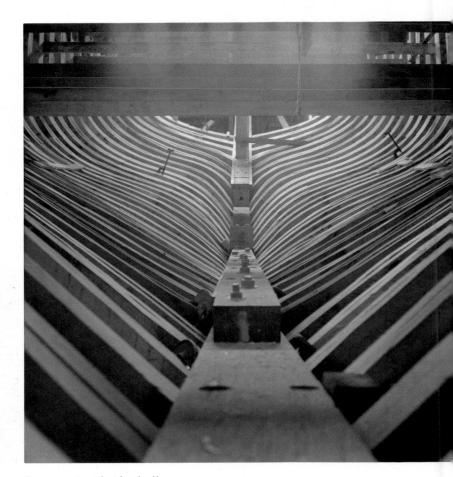

Framing inside the hull.

Planking nears completion.

Les Thompson caulking the hull.

Topsides

Launching, August 22, 1978.
Photo by Rev. Raymond F. Smith.

20

Underway

In the spring of 1978, the work on *Appledore*'s hull was only part of the round the world project. Having committed ourselves to this voyage, we placed advertisements in various magazines and newspapers seeking people to fill our twelve crew positions. By the beginning of April, we were deluged with hundreds of letters. For most people, the inquiries turned out to be extensions of a dream to do something adventurous in their lives. Many of these people knew they could never go because of health reasons, job commitments, lack of funds required to share in the expenses of the trip, or just plain lack of courage.

I personally talked with the small number of serious people to explain what their responsibilities would be. The most important consideration was the person's enthusiasm. Experience did not matter in the slightest. However, I wanted them to be aware of the hardships. This would not be a luxury vacation and there would be no passengers. Everyone would have to share in the work of sailing the vessel, raising and lowering sails, steering, and painting *Appledore*'s many wooded surfaces. The trip itself would not be easy. Living quarters would be cramped and we didn't have normal conveniences like showers, running water and refrigeration. It would be work just trying to get along with all the other crew members. Getting used to the motion of the boat was also a serious consideration. Everyone would probably feel seasickness at one time or another.

On November 9, 1978, *Appledore*'s crew consisted of fifteen people including my family and myself. The youngest member was my son, Tommy at 1 1/2-years old and the oldest was a couple in their mid 60's although later in the trip we would be joined by a gentleman who was 71-years old. At the onset, the women outnumbered the men eight to seven. I felt we had a good healthy cross section of individuals.

Meeting the November 9, 1978 deadline for departure was probably the most difficult obstacle we had to face. Although the Gamage shipyard had finished the hull on August 22, the interior, companionways and rigging were not completed. At the end of August, the masts were stepped and *Appledore* motored to Kittery, Maine. The outfitting began in Kittery with the help of six local boat builders and many volunteers who wished to contribute something to the trip even though they could not be a part of the crew.

At the same time, over 400 cases of canned food was ordered from several companies. Once the cans were delivered in mid October, the mad rush was on. All available hands were put to the task of unloading the cases and varnishing every can to prevent rusting. The inventory was amazing: 210 pounds of peanut butter, 3 cases of dehydrated apples, 15 cases of boned chicken, 95 pounds of honey, 1200 pounds of flour, 1050 rolls of toilet paper, 120 cans of Danish hams, and on and on. The next task was finding a place to put it all. Somehow we worked around the carpenters, who continued to nail bunks and shelves together, stuffing cans in the bilges, under bunks and generally wherever there was an open space.

To add to the confusion, as the day of departure approached, the crew began to move onboard stashing the two duffle bags of items allowed under bunks and into nets that swung everywhere from the bulkheads. With the threat of approaching winter upon us, we were forced to work well into the night to get *Appledore* in shape. Before we knew it however, November 9 had arrived and still the carpenters worked.

continued on page 24

Anchor light

Dusk brings cool relief on deck.

Doris and Tom

Underway off Moorea

At 3:00 p.m., we put an end to the loud hammering and the sound of buzzing saws and under the eyes of several hundred people and a cannon salute, *Appledore* slipped away from the dock. The explosion of the cannon reminded me of the sound one might hear at the finishing line of a race. For us, the most difficult work was over, we had won our race. It was time to forget about all the hectic hours and days of preparation and begin to think of the challenge ahead of sailing and learning to relax. A feeling of relief filled me as I left the mouth of the Piscataqua River and headed out to sea.

This passage would also be *Appledore*'s maiden voyage. I did not feel any qualms about beginning the trip with this unproven vessel. After all, the basic design had been proven during more than 100 years of use. Furthermore, for over one hundred and fifty years, American schooners had evolved and all the rigging and fitting specifications for *Appledore* had been taken from Howard Chapelle's book "The American Fishing Schooner." Also, I had been at the shipyard every day the Gamage crew worked on this incredibly strong vessel.

Repairing sails

John Richards bending on sail

Dave and Marion Dash

Haul out, American Samoa

Greg Wellstead

La Plaza island, Galapagos

Galapagos

Two months out of Portsmouth, after stops in Bermuda, Haiti, Jamaica and Panama, we reached the Galapagos Islands, the jumping off point for our trip through the Pacific. From here we would begin our longest straight sailing passage, 3,015 miles to the Marquesas islands in French Polynesia. More importantly though, the Galapagos was one of the expected highlights of the voyage.

Although we were unable to obtain written permission from the government of Ecuador to visit the islands, we decided to stop for fuel and water and hope for the best. Upon arrival at San Cristobal, we were informed that we would be allowed 72 hours to reprovision but we could not visit any other island. A little friendly persuasion and one teeshirt later, the officials relented and allowed us to spend 10 days on San Cristobal, Santa Cruz and La Plaza islands.

As I began to walk about the islands, I could imagine the excitement Darwin must have experienced when he visited the Galapagos in 1837. Prehistory seems to merge with the 20th century. On San Cristobal, I spent a day watching the sea iguanas skitter across the rocks, their black horny bodies barely descernable from the dark volcanic rocks. Seals were so friendly that you had to tuck in your toes in fear they they would give them a playful nip.

Santa Cruz is the home of the famous tortoises which rest lazily in the hot sun perhaps blinking an eyelid or two if they can find energy to do so. They seem to realize their VIP status on the island.

La Plaza island, a rock no larger than two square miles, was the best wildlife sanctuary of all. A large school of hammerhead sharks cruised near the island waiting to catch a sea lion from the largest sea lion colony in the islands. The sea lions let it be known from the start that they were in total command and they stubbornly refused to move and give us space to moor our boat. The aroma of half digested fish got stronger as they barked their protests. We would not have attempted to go ashore without our official guides. After determining that no bulls were near, we did manage to squeeze between two protesting pups.

Among the cliffs on the south side of the island, various species of birds were nesting, the most unusual being the blue footed boobies with their dazzling, baby blue webbed feet. The least timid creatures of all, however, were the land iguanas. They seemed to enjoy gawking at us as much as we did at them. After several minutes, a quick flick of their tongue gave us to understand that we were not worth considering. Not to be snubbed so easily, the guide offered them a cactus bud which they accepted with relish somehow managing to avoid the sharp quills.

Soon, I began to notice the slight trade wind breeze that was blowing gently over the island and realized with regret that our ten days were over.

Pilots boarding ship, Panama Canal

28

Appledore in the locks, Panama Canal, day after Christmas

Anchored off San Christobal, Galapagos

Tortoise, Santa Cruz, Galapagos

Land iguana,
La Plaza Island,
Galapagos

Tuna fishing fleet, American Samoa

South Pacific

The Pacific is the largest ocean in the world and that part called the South Pacific is supposed to be the calmest, although that is not always true. Here many a man, in the past and in the present, has sought paradise. The warm tropical water and trade winds provide a green house environment for the human body. If it is hot during the day, the cool breeze in the evening will reward any discomfort one may have had to bear.

On many islands, we came across individuals who had sought paradise in the manner of Robert Louis Stevenson and Paul Gauguin. One example was Bernard Moitessier, the famous French voyager and writer. At one time he participated in the around-the-world-single-handers' race sponsored by England's Sunday Times. He had the lead and was two-thirds of the way around the globe when he suddenly changed course. Instead of crossing the finish line and collecting the prize of 5,000 pounds sterling, Moitessier continued around the world a second time. Everyone speculated that he had gone mad. Friends could not even convince him to pull into a port. He headed back to the South Pacific where he lives today. I met him planting vegetables on a hill surrounded by trees swishing in the trade wind breeze. Small laughing children played close by and we were introduced to his lovely wife. We were later honored to have him come aboard *Appledore* for a visit. He is but one of many unusual people who live on the small secluded islands of the South Pacific.

In the Pacific, the distances between islands are often great. For instance, it is just over 3,000 miles to the Marquesas islands from the Galapagos. We were alone on the great stretch of ocean for twenty-three days. To observe porpoises frolicking under our bow was a great thrill and to see whales within a hundred feet of *Appledore*'s hull was even more exciting.

The seclusion of twenty-three days at sea did wonders for my sense of smell. As we approached the Marquesas, the tropical breeze carried the smell of land to us five to ten miles out. I breathed in deeply. Green vegetation lined the hills to relieve our empty horizon and coconut trees close in on shore waved to us in the morning breeze. We anchored in Fatu Hiva Bay where sheer cliffs rose up sharply supporting an abundance of plants and trees. This was paradise—a green house with a tinted blue glass dome overhead. After this long passage, I learned to appreciate the rich living hue of green.

Reef, Tahiti

34

Fatu Hiva, Marquesas Islands

Tahiti

Pentecost Island, New Hebrides

Tahiti, looking towards Moorea

Honiara, Guadalcanal, Solomon Islands

Darwin, Australia

Tahiti

Bali Mountain, Moorea

Tahiti

Tahiti

Pentecost Island,
New Hebrides

Cooks Bay, Moorea

Market, Bali, Indonesia

Indian Ocean

The distance from Darwin, Australia to Durban, South Africa is 5,600 miles. Our passage along this route was interrupted by Bali, Christmas Island, the Cocos (Keeling) Islands, Rodrigues, and Mauritious.

I had been told that Bali would be one of the most interesting places we would visit. The prediction was correct. Bali was a different world. This was the first example of the Asian culture we saw on the voyage. The island is divided between the Hindu and Moslem faiths. Temples abound everywhere from stone carvings of gods around the city to the sacred monkey forest where hundreds of grey monkeys live, their small wooded area centered by a beautiful Hindu temple.

The countryside is neatly terraced with rice fields. Water buffalo are harnessed to plow the fields and, as they have for centuries, women thrash the ripe rice by hand. In Bali, the twentieth century mingles in with the centuries past. Gasoline engines propel the taxis on the street but the wind alone powers the ferries from island to island.

We made our fastest passages on the Indian Ocean. There the trade winds fetch across thousands of miles of open water unbroken by any major land forms and the seas build to great heights. We covered 2,000 miles in *Appledore*'s record time of only ten and a half days. The long distances were broken up by stops at lonely islands far from the trouble of the world. We took shelter at uninhabited Direction island in the Cocos Island group. We relaxed there for three days before proceeding to Rodrigues island. It was not without some restlessness for me. Each night I could hear the loud pounding of the surf on the windward side of the island. Under the moonlight, I could see the coconut trees bending to 30-knot winds which sang a low mournful tune as it blew through the rigging. Soon we had to leave for the cyclone season would arrive and that would be no time to cross the Indian Ocean in a small sailboat. On that windy passage, we ate down below which was unusual for us as normally we ate on deck to get away from the heat. *Appledore* sailed very nicely with double reefed main sail, single reefed foresail and staysail. Our fastest day of the passage and the trip was 209 miles in 24 hours.

Indian Ocean

43

Ferry boat,
Benoa Harbor, Bali

Holy Monkey Forest, Bali

Temple, Bali

45

Bali rice fields

Market, Bali

Bali rice field

Direction Island, Cocos Islands

Giant water lilies, Mauritious

Christmas Island

Rodrigues Island

Market, Port Louis, Mauritious

50

Arriving Port Mathurin, Rodrigues Island

Howick Falls, South Africa

South Africa

South Africa is a port of call that has everything; spectacular views, friendly people and as many modern conveniences as the United States could offer. After spending a year in lesser developed countries, South Africa was a treat.

South Africa seems to have a touch of every type of view the world has to offer. A tropical belt lies in the area bordering the Indian Ocean. Palm trees wave their greeting to the world inviting people to enjoy the beautiful, warm water beaches. On the Atlantic side, the water is cold and the coast is graced by beautiful beaches and unusual rock formations that excite the viewer with a myriad of colors. Palm trees are replaced by a spectacle of wild flowers which come alive on the desert floor as far as the eye can see. On this side too, the mountains rise above Capetown, one of South Africa's major cities. Tabletop mountain which looms over the city is the local weather forecaster for the area. Whenever a gale is approaching, the flat mountain top is covered by clouds which cascade down the sides of the mountains earning it the name "tablecloth." When the tablecloth is set, a good strong gale can be expected. One can take a cable car to the top to watch the clouds build and tumble over each other. Other mountains offer ravines like the Grand Canyon and in some places waterfalls cascade down for some 260 feet.

Beyond the mountains stretch miles and miles of savanna grasslands and the horizon is unbroken except for scattered solitary trees.

The South African wildlife is as varied as the terrain. Elephants, lions, hyenas, herds of zebras and antelope, ostriches, giraffes, and baboons fill the 10 national parks. In other areas, the animals continue to roam free as they have for centuries.

The cities have much of interest too. Durban, our first port of call in South Africa, and Capetown, our port of demarcation across the Atlantic, were the cleanest, most picturesque cities we saw in the world. Capetown, as a cultural center, offered everything from opera to the Salvation Army Christmas carolers.

In order to travel from one city to the next, we had to sail around the Cape of Storms, better known as the Cape of Good Hope. The name, Cape of Storms, seems more fitting. The entire coast of South Africa must be considered one of the windiest, most treacherous shorelines on earth. We were fortunate to have hourly weather forecasts and thus were able to anticipate approaching gales. On our 820-mile passage from Durban to Cape Town, we had to duck into two different harbors of refuge to wait out a couple of 50-knot gales. Although we were able to sail in relatively calm airs, we never forgot that getting caught in a storm in that area of freak waves could put us in great danger. We were all relieved on the day we spotted the lighthouse at Cape Point, the most powerful beacon in the world. It marked the end of our passage around the Cape. Soon, we were safely tied up to a dock in Cape Town, where a couple of days later we rode out a gale that gusted to 70-mph.

After spending two months in South Africa, we still had other sights to see but finally the day came when we had to resume our voyage and cross the South Atlantic to the Caribbean.

Donna, arriving Cape Town

Durban Harbor, South Africa

54

Cape Town and Table Mountain

False Bay, South Africa

Cape Point, South Africa

56

South Coast, South Africa

Slangkopponi Light House, South Coast, South Africa

Howick River, South Africa

Thousands Hills Church, South Africa

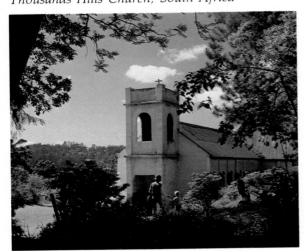

59

Baboons

*View from summit
of Table Mountain, Cape Town*

Lion in park

Giraffe

Owl

Cape of Good Hope Light House

Waterfall, South Africa

Cape Town freight yard

64

Saint Helena

South Atlantic

The trip across the South Atlantic represented to most of us the beginning of our homeward bound passage. We were returning to the Caribbean where only one year earlier we had visited the islands of Haiti and Jamaica.

After 15 relaxing days at sea, we arrived at St. Helena, the island where Napoleon was exiled after his capture by the British. Kipling reflects the British point of view in a poem:

How far is St. Helena from the fields of Waterloo?
A near way—a clear way—the ship will take you soon,
A pleasant place for gentlemen with little left to do!

Napoleon's conception of the island was far different. He hated the confines of St. Helena and its disagreeable climate and he disliked being kept under surveillance by captors no less disagreeable than the weather. In a house now restored as a museum, he lived a lonely, unhappy life until he died of stomach cancer in 1821. Although the island belongs to Britain, the small acreage upon which his house stands is French.

The main community on St. Helena is located in a narrow ravine, an odd place to build a town. When it rains, which is not often on this part of the island, the roads become rivers and are sometimes impassable. The town is located in an area so dry that cactus is the predominate foliage.

At higher elevations, where Napoleon's house is located, the hot arid land becomes green, lush and cool. Most of the island's food supply is grown or raised here among the mist shrouded hills. Once the island's major source of revenue, flax grows wild along the roadside and in the fields which are being stripped for grazing land now that synthetics have become the mainstay of rope production.

On descent from this heavenly area, one again is thrown into a hell of bareness, heat, and erosion. However, the colors exhibited in the gullies make one question what, in fact, beauty is. Like many other places we visited, St. Helena is an island of contrasts not only in terrain and climate, but also the effect it has on people. Although Napoleon could find little good about the island, I thought it was beautiful.

Four days sail from St. Helena is the sister island of Ascension. If Napoleon thought St. Helena was bad, he should have visited this small island.

NASA and the United States Air Force have long term leases on Ascension. NASA had built a tracking station on the island which is due to be replaced by a satelite in the near future. Ascension was the most restrictive island we visited. Yachts are allowed to stay only 72 hours and we were given a curfew. You had to be back onboard by 6:30 p.m., unless you were sponsored as we were, then we were asked to return by 11:00 p.m. The police are very firm. Violators are taken to jail and sent back to sea the following day.

Ascension has the most inhospitable terrain I have encountered anywhere in the world. It reminded me of pictures I had seen of the moon. Dry volcanic rocks, many in large fragments, cover the island. One piece took on the perfect form of a dinosaur. NASA's antennas pricked the barren landscape in hundreds of locations giving the area an even eerier look. It was chilling to learn that back in the 1800's, ships on their way back from Africa used Ascension as a dumpoff point for yellow fever victims. They would leave the sick in a cove aptly named Comfortless Cove. The few people on the island left food for the sick and if the people recovered, they could walk out. The dead were buried in the small cemetary located in a sort of bowl surrounded by spears of stone. I saw the names of four different ships, all dating back to the 1830's.

There was only one redeeming spot on the island—the 10 acres located at the top of its highest mountain. Here a small peak pushed above the horrors of the rest of the island. This area was green and cool. A large catchment had been built to collect drinking water because there are no rivers or well although, the United States has built a distillation plant.

It appeared that even the fish had taken on some of the characteristics of the island. All around the boat strange black scavenger fish swam waiting for a morsel of food to stray over the side. As if they realized the barrenness of the area, the fish accepted anything; banana peels, bread, whatever. Ironically, we found that fishing was as good here as anywhere that we had been with grouper and tuna in abundance. Seventy-two hours after arrival at Ascension we began a relatively easy sail to the Caribbean covering the 2400 miles in 17 days.

Jamestown, Saint Helena

Meadow, Saint Helena

67

(This page and opposite) Saint Helena's eroded landscape

68

69

Comfortless Cove, Ascension Island

Georgetown, Ascension Island

Green Mountain Farm, Ascension Island

Bonetta Cemetery, Comfortless Cove

Pitons, Saint Lucia

Caribbean

It was hard to believe that a year had elapsed since we had last been in the Caribbean. It seemed like yesterday that we were walking the streets of Jamaica and Haiti. Now our minds were no longer preoccupied with thoughts of the next port, instead we began to think about home and job possibilities. With the threat of change upon us it was difficult to relax and enjoy these beautiful islands with the same intensity we had seen the rest of the world. Many of us were anxious to get on with it and return to Portsmouth. The Lesser Antilles, that group of islands which extends from Trinidad to the Virgin Islands, are after all, in the United States' backyard.

Despite our feelings, we did enjoy visiting and seeing the diversity of these islands. Each island seems different from the next. The lower islands are dry and arid, cactus being the predominate vegetation. Yet the next island can be mountainous, wet and lush with very little sunlight able to penetrate the dense mass of leaves. The people also vary. These islands are populated almost entirely by people who had immigrated or who were sent here against their will. Almost all of the native population died long ago. Although the Negroid race dominates in the islands, there are many whites and Indians. The difference does not end here however. Some of the islands are French, others Dutch or English, each keeping its own customs, language, and governments.

It was a pleasant change to sail between ports less than 100 miles apart. Usually we would leave one island in the morning and be at the next island before dark. As ships did in the old sailing days, we used the Northeast trade winds to our advantage as we slowly made our way north. As we sailed up the chain we stopped at Trinidad, where we got to see the tail end of Carnival week, and at Grenada, still one of the biggest producers of nutmeg in the world. We were surprised to see half the charter yacht fleet anchored in Beguia, a small island belonging to St. Vincent, where the Caribbean's best maintained botanic gardens can be found.

We anchored between St. Lucia's famous Pitons enjoying the company of the Andrews family who run the coconut plantation there. The Pitons are two larva plugs over 2000 feet high which are the remains of an extinct volcano.

Martinique was as French as Paris. Small sidewalk cafes dotted the city. Wine and cheese filled half the grocery stores where beautiful women in the latest Parisian fashions, long loaves of French bread tucked under their arms, stood trying to select their next meal.

Dominica, a former English possession, was just beginning to recover from the devastation of hurricane David that struck the island in the summer of 1979. The people did not look defeated and certain spots of interest like Indian River and Trafalgar Falls retained much of their beauty despite the lack of foliage. Antigua's English Harbor was still the anchorage for millions of dollars worth of yachts. A low island, it was as dry as ever, the cactus on the hillside thriving above all other vegetation.

Barbuda's beaches were the most desolate yet beautiful of all. It was a pleasure to build a sand castle with Tom and know that its only destroyer would be nature itself. St. Barts is also French but much smaller than Martinique; the towns were quaint and lightly populated and its beaches are made of shells in some places a foot or two deep.

Saba was no less quaint; a Dutch town in miniature. This island is as unlike the rest of the Lesser Antilles as it could possibly be. A Dutch possession, Saba has no beaches. Cliffs

73

rise steeply all around the island making the roads, which were built mainly by hand, twist and turn like a corkscrew.

Our final stop in the Caribbean was St. Thomas in the U.S. Virgin Islands. There we began the slow transition back to life in America. We started by eating our first "Big Mac" and pizza since leaving the States. Grocery stores were filled with so many different kinds of food and different brands it made my head spin. I felt gorged just looking at it all. Cruise ships and tourists were everywhere. Was this what we wanted to go back to?

Saint Georges' Harbor, Grenada

Grenada

Concord Falls, Grenada

75

St. Lucia

76

Marigot Bay, St. Lucia

Falls, Dominica

78

Deep Bay, Antigua

Deep Bay, Antigua

Edward Grant, Antigua

Boat building, St. Johns, Antigua

Barbuda

Coco Beach, Barbuda

82

Gustavia Harbor, St. Barts

Saba

Saba

Nantucket Light Ship

North Atlantic and Home

As we approached the island of Bermuda, excitement filled the crew. We would be entering St. Georges, Bermuda in a matter of hours and nine out of the original crew of fifteen had made it all the way around the world. They survived without the convenience of running water, hot water, flush toilets, fresh water showers every day, blow dryers, hair dyes, air-conditioning, the family automobile, refrigeration, and television. They also succeeded in living in tight quarters surrounded by as many as 14 people during long stretches when we were at sea and the possibility of escaping on land was gone. I congratulate those nine people for having the fortitude to stick it out for the entire 18 months. The crew was probably closer in the minutes when we passed through St. George's narrow gut than at any other time on the entire trip. A feeling of accomplishment came over us and rightly so.

This was our second time in Bermuda since the trip began. Ironically, it was our first stop after leaving Portsmouth and it would be the final port before arriving home. We had not planned to visit here in November of 1978 but due to a small gale and a green crew we had pulled in. It is a good port to see more than once. The people are exceptionally friendly, there are great shops, beautiful sandy beaches, and incredible snorkling. It has all the ingredients of a super tourist community.

I had been asked by a newspaper man just before departing on the trip what day and time I would return to Portsmouth. Having answered about all the questions I could handle, I had shot back "May 17 at 2:30 p.m." Unfortunately, every day thereafter the proposed deadline kept cropping up in my mind. By the time the trip was half over, I was determined to make that deadline. We left Bermuda on May 10 allowing what I hoped would be one extra day.

The North Atlantic is one of the roughest areas of ocean in the world. In fact, our worst weather has always been experienced there. The Gulf Stream, a warm water current which travels thousands of miles from the Gulf of Mexico to Europe, courses its way from only a few miles to a couple of hundred miles away from the North American coast. In order to travel from the continent to Bermuda, one must cross the current, which flows northward as fast as 4 knots. When the gales, which frequently blow off the Virginia Capes hit the Gulf Stream, terrible sea conditions are produced. Without warning, irregular seas build up to 20 feet or more. When the warm and cold air masses clash, severe thunder storms are produced. Our first passage from Portsmouth to Bermuda had been rough, a small gale of 30 knots forcing the seas to pile up to 10 feet. It was not a severe storm but one that made us physically uncomfortable due to the rolling and pitching of the vessel. We expected no better on this passage. However, we were greatly surprised by the relatively calm clear weather we experienced on the entire passage back to Portsmouth. It was as if Mother Nature was acknowledging *Appledore*'s accomplishment.

One day out of Portsmouth and three miles off Cape Ann, Massachusetts, we witnessed the best wildlife show of the entire trip. Hundreds of porpoises suddenly appeared leaping and diving about the boat. Off in the distance, we could see large sprays of water shooting into the sky and then the incredible view of a huge tail raising above the water's surface only to disappear moments later. Within minutes, a pod of some six to seven whales approached *Appledore*, their enormous bodies rising and falling over the swells. The whales were as long as the boat giving some concern as to whether they would hit us or not. Incredibly, just as collisions seemed eminent, they would slowly but gracefully plunge down to deeper depths. For most of us this was our welcome home committee. Our families and friends in Portsmouth would be hard pressed to beat the whale's act.

May 17, 1980 arrived. At 8:00 a.m., we were sailing again among the Isles of Shoals. As we slowly began to make our way toward the mouth of the Piscataqua River, we heard a call, on channel 16 on our ship-to-shore radio, from the Coast Guard to Schooner *Appledore*. The news was out. Within a half hour, three sail boats joined us, one vessel firing a salute with a small brass cannon mounted on its stern. Another vessel came close enough to toss us a bouquet of apple blossoms. As we got nearer, more boats surrounded us, horns blaring and cannons firing. At the mouth of the harbor, the Coast Guard approached with a 40-footer and dropped off an officer and a customs official. I had wondered what clearing customs would entail. Some people have experienced nightmares but we were welcomed by a friendly, courteous man who cleared us within a half hour.

Our official work complete, we headed down past the naval prison, the excitement and emotion of the moment almost overwhelming. My eyes were on the clock, 2:15 p.m. It was time to travel the final distance beneath the outstretched arms of the Memorial Bridge. We did not need to call them to raise the middle span of the bridge. The noise and commotion of the large flotilla of boats accompanying us was enough. Again, the horns were blaring and the cannon firing. All along the sidewalk of the bridge, hundreds of people strained to give a welcoming shout. Banners welcomed *Appledore* home.

We sailed smoothly under the bridge, full sail set and drawing. Hundreds of people lined the bank and lawns on Badger's Island where *Appledore* would finally come to rest. For the last time the sails were dropped, no one quite realizing the finality of the act, everyone being overwhelmed with the emotions of seeing old friends and families. Moments later we approached the docks and tied our lines to the pilings. At last, the gangway was raised and my wife and son started the parade ashore. Thank God we had made it home safe and sound, and only 17 seconds before 2:30 p.m. For all of us, it was on to new adventures.

Gregg Wellstead at the wheel with Donna and Alan Twombly.

Bermuda

Dolphins, off Cape Ann, North Atlantic

North Atlantic

Hauling sails, St. Thomas

90

Portsmouth, New Hampshire

*Appledore in
Portsmouth Harbor
Photo by Rev. Raymond F. Smith.*

91

Appendix I

The following comments are offered to sailors who are contemplating a voyage similar to the one made by Appledore. It is not possible to provide all of the details for such a trip but hopefully these comments will assist in planning an undertaking as complicated as a round the world voyage.

There are good and bad seasons to cross any ocean. Just as the four seasons of New England are noticeably different, so too are the seasons of the sea. On this voyage, we planned to sail during summer, the calmest and safest season for each of the oceans.

Once a route has been determined, the most immediate purchase should be charts. United States, British and French charts are all excellent and they should be ordered several months in advance. As a precaution, order extra charts in the event you have to make an unscheduled stop. Also, it is difficult to obtain charts outside the United States, so don't expect to buy charts enroute.

Visas, which at first seemed very important, we learned later were impractical to secure before departure as most would expire before arrival in the country applied to. If planning to visit Indonesian waters, it is essential to contact the American embassy in Jakarta eight months to a year in advance. They will send back a form which must be filled out and returned with a deposit of $30 for a cruising permit for Indonesian waters such as Bali. This is not to be confused with a personal visa, this permit is for the vessel. Personal visas must be obtained also but are easier to get in New Guinea or Australia as long as the vessel's permit has been acquired. This requirement should not be taken lightly. Governments of many third world countries make laws which change from week to week and seem harsher than laws in larger, more developed countries. Once in their waters, they reign as king and it is easier and safer to bend to the rules than to argue.

Of course, in every port a passport is required and customs must be cleared before anyone can go ashore.

A cruising permit is also required to visit the Galapagos Islands. It must be obtained through the Ecuadorian Navy in Washington. The permit is difficult to obtain. After a year of red tape and waiting, the permit might not be granted. Without a permit, vessels are limited to a visit of 72 hours to replenish supplies at San Cristobal Island. It may be possible to anchor at Santa Cruz Island and, for a fee, join a tour group with Ecuadorian guides on Ecuadorian boats.

South Africa requires visas before entering the country. In this case, get the visa in advance because many countries en route have broken off relations with South Africa and there are few places to obtain visas. The South African visa is good for twelve months. Ports can still be entered without the visa but crews are restricted to the city limits unless a $1,000 cash bond is posted.

A similar bond is also required in French Polynesia if the visit is more than 30 days. The money is refundable in both cases. These bonds are not meant to inconvenience visitors but to assure officials that people will have money enough to get passage home and not be marooned there.

Smallpox vaccinations are still required in some ports despite what your local doctor may say, therefore, get an international immunization book and spend some extra time and money to get every shot available. Before departure, my son, Tommy, and everyone else had shots for yellow fever, cholera, smallpox, typhoid, polio and tetanus. Fortunately no one had any of these diseases. Cholera needs a booster every six months and one can be obtained almost anywhere. Malaria tablets are suggested and everyone on board took them, especially if they planned to visit the interior of many countries. In Australia, crews are asked to take a series of tablets to insure malaria isn't carried into the country. Our young son did not take them but we were very careful to keep him away from mosquito infested areas. If at all possible, get flavored tablets or liquid medicine for children. It is almost impossible to get these bitter tablets down a young child's throat.

One of the most important and essential things to bring is money. American currency loses its value up to 30 percent in many ports and money flows like water on a voyage of this nature. If a port visit is longer than 10 days, money can be wired from the States. Credit cards are convenient too. In the South Pacific, Visa and American Express seem to be widely used. In South Africa and the Caribbean, Master Charge and Visa predominate. Cash in small bills appeals to me if it is carefully stored and there is always someone on board the vessel as there was on *Appledore*. Travelers checks are fine but can become a real nuisance to cash in some ports—have plenty of identification.

Port fees have increased considerably. In comparison to a previous voyage to the West Indies, the fees have gone up as much as 50 percent in five years. The worse encounter was in French Guiana. The officials were not convinced that I was a pleasure yacht, therefore, my port fees were $750. In the Galapagos, we paid $67, and in Guadalcanal the fee was $132 for a two day stay. In French Polynesia, fees were reasonable. A total of one month's port fees came to $57. Australia and South Africa are free for the first 30 days as are many other ports. In the Lesser Antilles, things have caught on and port fees are generally $20 to $40 for each port. All these port fees apply to a vessel in yacht status and not to one in the commercial charter trade.

Small yachts do not require a pilot—beware if someone tells you it is necessary. Sometimes pilot's fees are up to $500 one way.

Most of our supplies were bought in the United States. It is wise to stock up with as much as possible. Certain items such as toilet paper, are not only expensive in some ports but almost impossible to get.

Doris, who did the provisioning, found it best to purchase the majority of our food through a local foods distributor which in our case was Monarch. The quality of this brand is excellent. Canned meats are particularly important as the availability, price, and quality of fresh meats in many ports is questionable. We bought canned beef chunks, boned chicken, hams, tuna, salmon and corned beef. All of these items are versatile. We did have trouble with certain meat salads such as ham and chicken salads. Items premixed with mayonnaise are not always good. Dehydrated apples, eggs, celery, and peppers were good but we did not need food prepared in this manner. Our source for dehydrated food was Bernard foods in Illinois and to a much lesser extent, Stow-a-Way foods in Boston. If you have not tasted certain products before ordering, try to get the company to send you a sample. It may save you a lot of money. We also bought many pounds of items such as peanuts and wheat germ from a natural foods company, but in a trip of this kind they were impractical. In the tropics preservatives are required or else hundreds of air tight containers are needed. Do not buy flour, in substantial amounts. After four months, we began to get weevils and without a freezer, we could not get rid of them without tossing the bags overboard.

There are several ways to protect cans. We found the best method was to varnish them, first removing the paper labels. Mayonnaise can be a real problem without refrigeration. After a day an open jar is unusable. Therefore, the use of the smallest jars available is a great help. Eggs can be kept as long as a month by coating them with vaseline and constantly turning them over. Powdered eggs are useful at sea and can be used in place of fresh eggs in baked goods.

Outside the United States, provisioning if planned correctly in advance can be relatively inexpensive. If most goods are purchased en route, expect to pay at least double and sometimes triple United States prices. The best ports we found for provisioning are as follows in order of direction traveled: Panama, American Samoa, Fiji, Australia, Mauritious (excellent vegetable market only), Africa, and St. Thomas, Virgin Islands.

There are several ports along the way where a vessel could be hauled out and repairs made. Our first haul out was in Panama where the tides are 18 feet and better. On the island of Tobago on the Balboa side of the Canal, there is a old dock where *Appledore* was grounded out. We had ample time between tides to scrub and paint the hull, although ground swells can be a problem.

American Samoa was another good port to haul out. It is advisable to make an appointment as they are usually very busy hauling fishing boats. We found the yard to be safe and very reasonable in cost. They can do just about any job required with wood or steel.

The Darwin, Australia, Yacht Club has a slipway, however, *Appledore* was too large to make use of it. Mauritious was probably the best port to haul out. The slipway owners in Port Louis treated yachts like royalty. They will give all the assistance they can with very reasonable rates. There is a waiting list so allow yourself a couple of extra weeks. Due to the time factor, we did not haul out there but the people who did had nothing but praise.

Capetown, South Africa was our third and final port to haul out. Again, the ways are safe and the cost reasonable. There are several railways in the Caribbean including GYS in Grenada and English Harbor, Antigua. Their prices compare with the United States, but they don't allow you to do your own work.

Sailmakers were few and far between and the quality of the work was questionable at best. We found the best solution to sail repairs was to buy a hand operated sewing machine and do our own work. Several other captains did likewise. The key to success is a super heavy needle and dacron thread, but both items are hard to find outside the United States. If new sails are needed as we required after a year of heavy wear and tear on our flax main and foresail, it is best to have the sails made in the States and then shipped to a reliable port. Most of the engine and toilet parts were difficult if not impossible to find outside the United States. Again we had them shipped to us from the United States. Give the package more than ample time to arrive. The more common items such as rope, buckets or wood can be obtained in any of the haul out ports.

Labor in many ports such as Haiti, Bali, or the West Indies is very inexpensive. There will be many requests for jobs. In these ports, by selecting a man carefully, much deck work can be completed.

There are of course certain ports to avoid if supplies or work are required. Most of the problem lies with the devaluation of the dollar. All the French ports are super expensive. A dozen eggs, for example, will cost upwards of $3. Any items which must be imported to an island will double in price and be difficult to find. We tried to be self-sufficient in all ways; food, parts, charts, etc., so that we could take advantage of the more inexpensive ports.

After an 18-month voyage and stops at 60 ports I have reached one firm conclusion. In comparison to what many countries have to offer, the United States has the most.

Table of Time and Distance

Ports of Call	Distance	Arrived	Departed
Portsmouth, New Hampshire	———	———	11/9/78
St. Georges, Bermuda	710 miles	11/15/78	11/27/78
Fort Liberte, Haiti	830 miles	12/5/78	12/6/78
Cap Haitien, Haiti	23 mi.	12/6/78	12/9/78
Port Royal, Jamaica	321 mi.	12/11/78	12/18/78
Colon, Panama	546 mi.	12/21/78	12/26/78
Balboa, Panama	48 mi.	12/26/78	12/29/78
Toboga Island, Panama	9 mi.	12/29/78	1/3/79
Flamenco Island, Panama	8 mi.	1/3/79	1/6/79
San Cristobal, Galapagos	870 mi.	1/12/79	1/15/79
Santa Cruz, Galapagos	43 mi.	1/15/79	1/18/79
La Plaza Islands, Galapagos	15 mi.	1/18/79	1/20/79
Santa Cruz, Galapagos	15 mi.	1/20/79	1/22/79
Hiva Oa, Marquesas Islands	3015 mi.	2/14/79	2/19/79
Fatu Hiva, Marquesas Islands	45 mi.	2/19/79	2/22/79
Taiohae Bay, Nuka Hiva, Marquesas	127 mi.	2/23/79	2/24/79
Ahe, Tuamotu	500 mi.	3/1/79	3/3/79
Papeete, Tahiti	280 mi.	3/6/79	3/16/79
Cooks Bay, Moorea	16 mi.	3/16/79	3/22/79
Huahine	85 mi.	3/23/79	3/26/79
Bora Bora	52 mi.	3/26/79	4/2/79
Rarotonga, Cook Islands	570 mi.	4/7/79	4/19/79
Pago Pago, Samoa	750 mi.	4/26/79	5/12/79
Apia, Western Samoa	75 mi.	5/13/79	5/17/79
Suva, Fiji	660 mi.	5/22/79	5/31/79
Efate, New Hebrides	610 mi.	6/4/79	6/9/79
Havannah Harbor, Efate	11 miles	6/9/79	6/10/79
Foreland, Epi, Island, New Hebrides	58 mi.	6/10/79	6/11/79
Pentecost, New Hebrides	50 mi.	6/11/79	6/20/79
Honiara, Guadalcanal, Solomon Is.	670 mi.	6/20/79	6/28/79
Port Moresby, New Guinea	900 mi.	7/4/79	7/14/79
Darwin, Australia	1050 mi.	7/21/79	8/9/79
Benoa, Bali, Indonesia	960 mi.	8/18/79	8/29/79
Christmas Island, Indian Ocean	590 mi.	9/2/79	9/8/79
Direction Island, Cocos Islands	520 mi.	9/11/79	9/15/79
Rodrigues Island	2000 mi.	9/26/79	10/3/79
Port Louis, Mauritious	380 mi.	10/6/79	10/13/79
Durban, South Africa	1560 mi.	10/25/79	11/28/79
East London, South Africa	258 mi.	11/30/79	12/1/79
Port Elizabeth, South Africa	131 mi.	12/2/79	12/4/79
Capetown, South Africa	425 mi.	12/7/79	12/29/79
Saint Helena Island	1697 mi.	1/12/80	1/16/80
Ascension Island	707 mi.	1/22/80	1/26/80
Cayenne, French Guiana	2400 mi.	2/12/80	2/14/80
Port-of-Spain, Trinidad	700 mi.	2/19/80	2/25/80
Saint Georges, Grenada	102 mi.	2/26/80	3/1/80
Tyrell Bay, Carriacou	30 mi.	3/1/80	3/2/80
Admiralty Bay, Bequia	35 mi.	3/2/80	3/4/80
Young Island, St, Vincent	8 mi.	3/4/80	3/6/80
Saint Lucia	55 mi.	3/6/80	3/13/80
Fort-de-France, Martinique	37 mi.	3/13/80	3/19/80
St. Pierre, Martinique	13 mi.	3/19/80	3/20/80
Roseau, Dominica	35 mi.	3/20/80	3/23/80

continued on next page

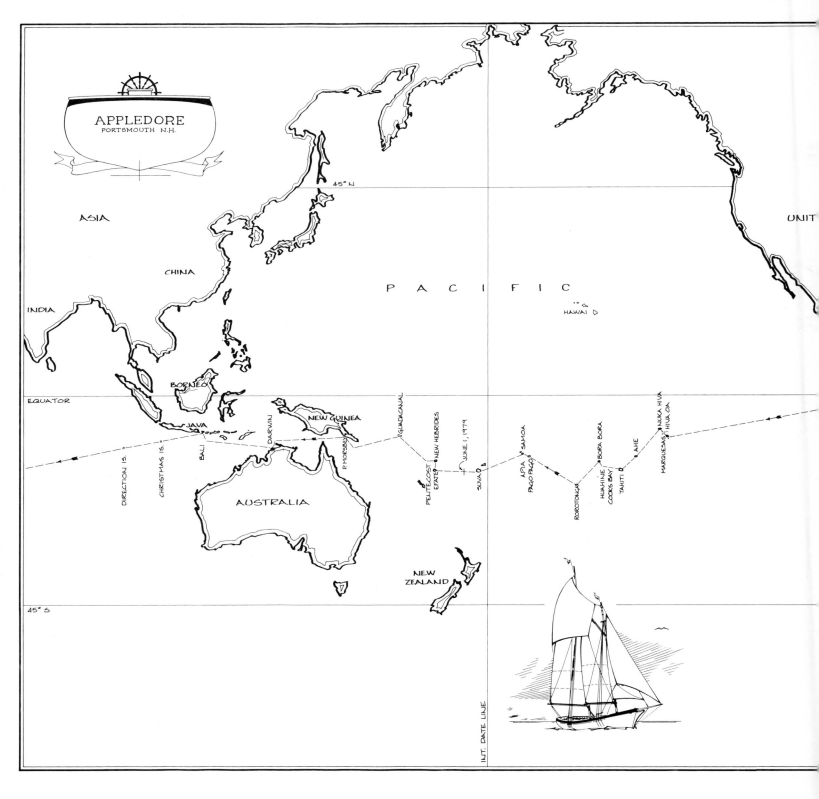

Portsmouth, Dominica	18 mi.	3/23/80	3/26/80
Deshayes, Guadeloupe	48 mi.	3/26/80	3/27/80
English Harbor, Antigua	42 mi.	3/27/80	4/6/80
St. John's, Antigua	20 mi.	4/8/80	4/9/80
Barbuda	30 mi.	4/9/80	4/12/80

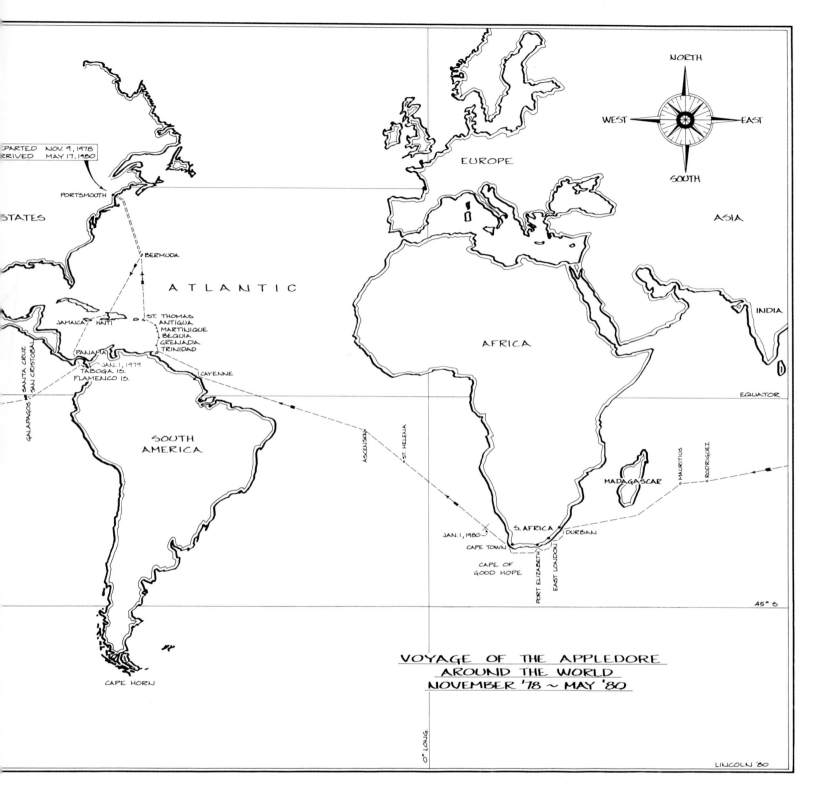

DEPARTED NOV. 9, 1978
ARRIVED MAY 17, 1980

PORTSMOUTH

STATES

BERMUDA

A T L A N T I C

JAMAICA HAITI
ST. THOMAS
ANTIGUA
MARTINIQUE
BEQUIA
GRENADA
TRINIDAD

PANAMA
JAN. 1, 1979
TABOGA IS.
FLAMENCO IS.

CAYENNE

SANTA CRUZ
SAN CRISTOBAL
GALAPAGOS

SOUTH
AMERICA

CAPE HORN

NORTH

WEST   EAST

SOUTH

EUROPE

ASIA

AFRICA

INDIA

EQUATOR

ASCENSION

ST. HELENA

MADAGASCAR

MAURITIUS

RODRIGUEZ

JAN. 1, 1980

S. AFRICA   DURBAN

CAPE TOWN

CAPE OF
GOOD HOPE   PORT ELIZABETH   EAST LONDON

45° S

0° LONG.

VOYAGE OF THE APPLEDORE
AROUND THE WORLD
NOVEMBER '78 ~ MAY '80

LINCOLN '80

St. Barts	68 mi.	4/12/80	4/17/80
Saba	30 mi.	4/17/80	4/20/80
St. Thomas, Virgin Islands	108 mi.	4/21/80	4/27/80
Bermuda	862 mi.	5/3/80	5/10/80
Portsmouth, New Hampshire	710 mi.	5/17/80	

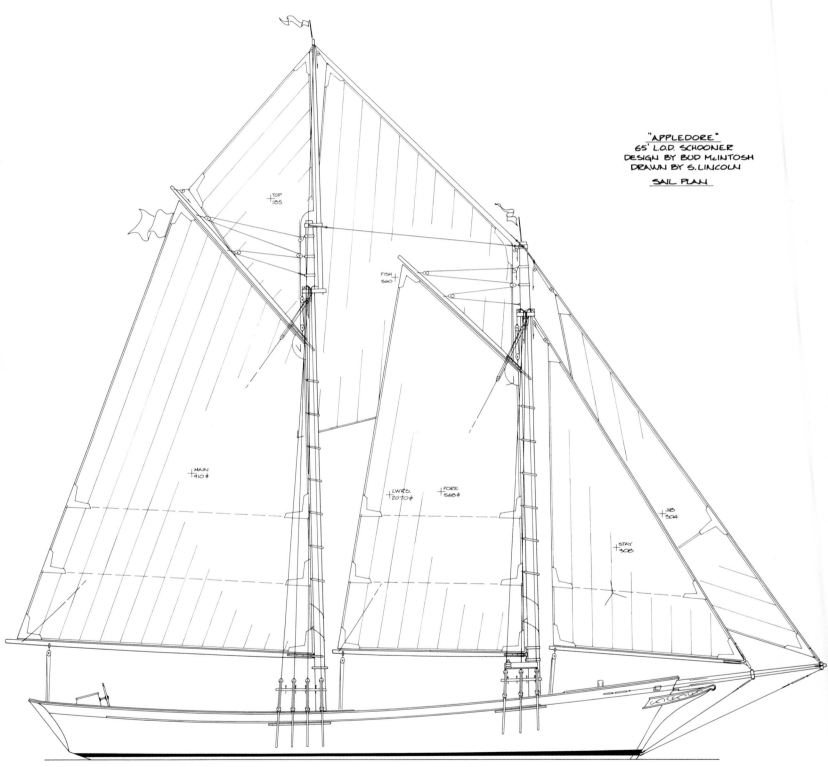

"APPLEDORE"
65' L.O.D. SCHOONER
DESIGN BY BUD McINTOSH
DRAWN BY S. LINCOLN

SAIL PLAN

TOP
185

FISH
560

MAIN
910#

LWRS.
2070#

FORE
548#

JIB
304

STAY
308

98

Schooner Appledore

A gaff rigged topsail schooner

Year built...1978
Designer...Bud McIntosh
Drafting and Consultant...Spencer Lincoln
Builder..Linwood Gamage, Gamage Shipyard
Captain...Herbert Smith
Length overall...82 feet
Length on deck..65 feet
Length along waterline...53 feet
Beam...18 feet 9 inches
Draft..9 feet 6 inches
Outside ballast (cast iron)...21,000 lbs.
Inside ballast...8,000 lbs.
Displacement...52 tons
Fuel capacity...200 gallons
Fresh water capacity..300 gallons

Scantlings

Keel...12 in. sided 10 in. molded
Keelson...8 in. sided 8 in. molded
Stem..10 in. sided 14 in. molded
Sternpost.......................................10 in. sided 17 in. molded
Horn timber.....................................10 in. sided 10 in. molded
Double sawn frames.............................3½ in. sided 8 in. molded
Deck beams.......................................4 in. sided 6 in. molded
Mast partners....................................6 in. sided 6 in. molded

Outside Planking

Garboards and bottom strakes.........................2 in. white oak
Topsides and bilges....................................2 in. fir
Butt blocks..2½ in. locust
Covering boards.....................................2 in. white pine
Deck..2 in. white cedar
Fastenings.........................Wrought iron and low carbon steel

Bulwarks

Stanchions..................................4 in. by 4 in. locust
Boards.......................................1½ in. white pine
Capping......................................1½ in. white oak

Inside Planking

Shelf.......................................3 in. sided by 9 in. molded
Clamp......................................2 in. sided by 12 in. molded
Bulkheads..2 in. pine
Ceiling...2 in. white pine
Cabins..White pine with oak trim

Auxiliary Diesel

Lehman Ford 254 cu. in. 80 h.p. with Warner 2.57 reduction
Propeller....................................3 bladed 23 in. by 13 in.

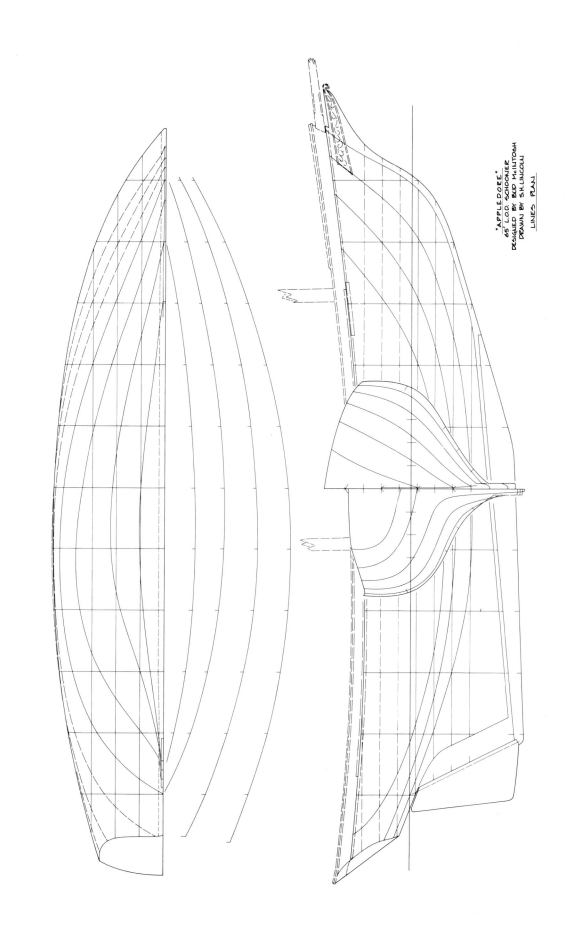

"APPLEDORE"
65' L.O.D. SCHOONER
DESIGNED BY BUD McINTOSH
DRAWN BY S.H. LINCOLN

LINES PLAN

Appledore underway.

Maggie doing needlepoint

Sandy sunbathing

Appledore anchored off Huahine, French Polynesia